LEARNING

To Fly

A Collection of Inspirational Stories

ANDI WHITEFIELD

ISBN 978-1-64079-517-4 (Paperback)
ISBN 978-1-64079-518-1 (Digital)

Christian Faith Publishing, Inc.
296 Chestnut Street
Meadville, PA 16335
www.christianfaithpublishing.com

Printed in the United States of America

I dedicate this book to my Lord and Savior Jesus Christ. He is always showing me that although I'm small, He is infinitely great! I can do all things through Christ, who strengthens me (Phil 4:13). I would also like to thank my cherished family and friends who encouraged me to write this book. You all enrich and bless my life every day.

Contents

PREFACE

*L*earning to fly.

Throughout my life, I have asked many times in prayer, "But, Lord, what if I fall?"

One day I heard Him softly whisper, "Oh, but my, beautiful one, what if you fly?"

In Isaiah 40:31, scripture tells us this: "But those who hope in the Lord will renew their strength. They will soar on wings like eagles; they will run and not grow weary, they will walk and not be faint."

So comes this collection of inspirational short stories. I pray that you will hear the loving voice of God through these stories and scriptures. My hope is that we all learn to trust God and allow Him to take us to new heights that we could never imagine on our own. I pray that as followers of Jesus Christ, we all learn to fly.

May the Lord answer you when you are in distress; may the name of the God of Jacob protect you. May he send you help from the sanctuary and grant you support from Zion. May he remember all your sacrifices and accept your burnt offerings. May he give you the desire of your heart and make all your plans succeed. May we shout for joy over your victory and lift up our banners in the name of our God. May the Lord grant all your requests. Now this I know: The Lord gives victory to his anointed. He answers him from his heavenly sanctuary with the victorious power of his right hand. (Ps 20:1–6)

God is faithful, who has called you into fellowship with his Son, Jesus Christ our Lord. (Cor 1:9)

HELLO, BEAUTIFUL!

One beautiful spring day, I decided to take a walk in the park. As I walked along the path, I saw the beauty of God's earth beginning to awaken from its long winter's nap. I was reminded of the verse from Ecclesiastes 3:11: "He has made everything beautiful in its time." I breathed in the fresh air as my eyes settled on the patches of green grass, budding trees, and tender spring flowers all stretching toward the sun.

As the path turned, I saw an elderly woman sitting on a bench. She smiled and said, "Hello." She asked me if I could sit with her for a moment or two.

I felt sorry for her, so I said sure. She had beautiful blue eyes, and when she looked at me, she tilted her head and smiled.

She was holding a lavender-colored handbag on her lap. I told her that I liked it, and she asked me if I would like to see some of her treasures inside. I politely said, "Of course."

The first item she pulled out was a tube of light-pink lipstick. She proudly stated that she put it on every day. She said that it helped her to remember to share things.

I asked her, "What sort of things?"

Then she quoted Hebrews 13:15–16, which says, "Through Jesus, therefore, let us continually offer to God a sacrifice of praise—the fruit of lips that confess His name. And do not forget to do good and to share with others, for with such sacrifices God is pleased."

I was beginning to realize that this was no ordinary woman. She explained that her lipstick helped her remember to use her lips to give thanks and praise to God and to share God's love with others. She quickly applied some of her lipstick to her lips and returned it to her handbag.

Then she began rummaging for the next item, which turned out to be a small bottle of perfume. She sprayed some of it into the air. It smelled like a bouquet of spring blossoms. She told me that as followers of Jesus Christ, we are a sweet aroma to God and to others. She stated that the perfume reminded her to always be that sweet aroma to others in her actions and words. She informed me that I could find that scripture in 2 Corinthians 2:15. I asked her if she had a Bible verse for every item in her handbag.

She giggled and said, "Almost!" She put her perfume away and began searching for something else.

Next, she held up a one-dollar bill. She said, "This one-dollar bill reminds me that I'm rich!"

I said, "Well that's nice."

She looked at me and said, "Oh, not by the world's standards."

She stated that she was rich by the kingdom's standards. She informed me 2 Corinthians 8:9 tells us, "For you know the grace of our Lord Jesus Christ, that though He was rich, yet for your sakes He became poor, so that you through His poverty might become rich."

She also spoke of Romans 8:14–17, which says, "Those who are led by the Spirit of God are sons and daughters of God. And by Him we cry, 'Abba Father.' The Spirit himself testifies with our spirit that we are God's children. Now if we are children, then we are heirs—heirs of God and co-heirs with Christ."

She smiled and said, "That tells me that I am rich with inheritance from God the Father."

She told me that her inheritance never ran out. She marveled that whatever she had used the day before would be replenished and waiting to be lavished on her the next day. I told her that I had never thought of myself as rich with God's inheritance.

She patted my hand and said, "Honey, you are if you know Christ as your Lord and Savior."

She told me that we as Christians should always collect on our daily inheritance from the Lord every single day, because He expects it! He gave His one and only Son to die for us just so we could have his glorious inheritance. She wrapped the dollar bill tight in her fragile hand and, pulling it to her chest, she said, "Thank you, God, for making me rich!"

After a few seconds of rummaging in her handbag again, the lady took out a small mirror. She turned it toward herself and peered in it. She traced one of the deep lines that ran down her face with her finger. Smiling at her reflection, she said, "Hello, beautiful."

I couldn't help smiling as her eyes twinkled and her face shined with joy. She told me that is what the Lord called her all the time. She said, "I know that to you I'm a tired and wrinkled old woman. But to Him I'm a beautiful, rare gem, and I get more beautiful with every passing day."

She shared with me that some mornings when she awoke she could hear His tender voice, saying,

"Good morning, beautiful. What kind of fun can we have today?"

She stated that in 2 Corinthians 4:16, scripture says, "Therefore we do not lose heart. Though outwardly we are wasting away, yet inwardly we are being renewed day by day."

She said, "Honey, the Lord assures us of our beauty to Him no matter what our size, shape, color, or age."

She also quoted Song of Songs 4:7, which says, "All beautiful you are, my darling; there is no flaw in you." She smiled in the mirror one more time and then put it away.

Her next items that she retrieved from the lavender handbag were two lacey and delicate handkerchiefs. She told me that one was for herself, and the other one was for anyone in need of comfort. She told me that when she was sad and tearful, she would get out her hanky and dry her tears. She smiled and told me that the Lord collects every tear and keeps record of them. I told her that I never knew that.

She shared Psalms 56:8, which says, "You keep track of all my sorrows. You have collected all my tears in your bottle. You have recorded each one in your book."

She said, "Oh, sweetie, this verse has comforted me so many times in my life. I know that God is with me, and He is lovingly collecting all of my tears. Not one of them falls that He does not know about."

A beautiful feather was her next choice. She smiled and asked me if I had any idea what the feather represented. I told her that I didn't have a clue. In Psalm 91:4, she told me that it says, "God will cover you with His feathers, and under His wings you will find refuge; His faithfulness will be your shield and rampart."

I told her that I didn't know what the word *rampart* even meant. She explained to me that it was a huge defensive wall that surrounds and protects. She stated that God surrounds us completely with His protection. She told me that the little feather reminded her that the Lord has every situation covered. He is always faithful and protects us.

The lady told me that she had one last item from her handbag to show me. She held up a half of a ticket stub. I told her that it looked interesting. She told me that when she looked at the ticket stub, it gave her hope and true excitement. She explained that in her mind she pictured Jesus having the other half with Him in heaven. When she arrived there one day, it will be a perfect match to hers. They will celebrate and hug, and Jesus will invite her into the lovely place that has been reserved for her.

She asked me if I had my own ticket stub. I told her that Jesus was my Savior, so yes, I did have my own stub as well. She clapped her hands together and said, "Wonderful, everyone should have a ticket!"

She told me that she just didn't understand why people don't want their free ticket. I told her that I didn't understand it either. She quoted 2 Peter 3:9: "God is patient with you, not wanting anyone to perish, but everyone to come to repentance." She put her ticket back inside her handbag still mumbling to herself and zipped it up.

"Well," she said, "what did you think of my treasures?"

I told her that I thought that they were all lovely and that she was lovely too. Smiling, she thanked me for my kind words.

She leaned back on the bench and said, "How wonderful it is to be so lovely to the Lord." She told me never to forget how lovely I was to Him.

She said, "Honey, I hope that you always allow Him to shine through you. One thing that I've learned through the years is that a person never knows when Jesus is going to need them to be beautiful for someone."

She quoted Ecclesiastes 3:11: "He has made everything beautiful in its time." She told me that throughout our lifetime He will make us beautiful in our own appointed times. It may be through our words, actions, deeds, or even through prayer for others. She encouraged me to always be ready!

She exclaimed, "Oh, what a blessing it is when your time to be beautiful is made known, and others are blessed through your obedience to God!"

I thanked her for her advice, and we said good-bye. I walked away with a little spring in my step and a renewed strength. I turned and looked over my shoulder, and I could see the woman still sitting on the bench. Someone else had walked by, and she had invited them to sit for just a moment or two. I thought to myself who would have ever known that the little elderly woman with the lavender handbag would have been such a blessing to me today! Then Ecclesiastes 3:11 came to my mind again: "God makes everything beautiful in its time." I was glad that God had made her beautiful that day just for me.

Christian, awaken from your long winter's nap and look up to the Son. Be blessed as He shines on and through you. His beauty in you will comfort, heal, and bless others.

THE WOOD FLOOR

Underneath a sink in my house there was an unfortunate leak. Water sprayed from a bad connection for about two weeks before I noticed. As I was walking through the dining room one day, I stepped on a slightly raised plank of wood. To my horror and shock, I soon realized what had happened. I found where the water was coming from and turned off the valve. The water had leaked under the wall and under the floor, causing it to buckle.

Each day the wood continued to buckle more and more. I called in the experts, and I was told that the floor would have to be replaced. I tried to stay calm and not stress myself out because I knew that this was going to be one big mess!

I said, "Okay, Lord, please help me to learn something from this experience. Is there something valuable that I can share with others?"

Time passed, and contractors were hired. As I was looking at the floor one day and trying to figure out where I would store the furniture during demolition, I had this thought about the water under the floor. On the surface the floor looked okay for a while with the water flowing underneath it. But soon the results of that water caused the floor to change.

That's what happens to us when we become Christians. When we accept Jesus as Savior and Lord, His living water flows through us. We are forever changed. In John 7:38, Jesus tells us that "whoever believes in Me as the scripture has said, streams of living water will flow from within him."

Jesus also tells us in John 4:4 that "the water I give will become in you a spring of water welling up to eternal life." As we deepen our relationship with God through daily prayer and Bible study, we become more aware of what He is telling us. What we don't realize is that just like the water reached every inch of the dark and unseen places under the wood floor, the living water of Jesus also reaches all of our dark and unseen places. We may not even realize that those places exist until He shows us.

What I am still discovering is the closer I become to Jesus, the more He shows me things in my life that are unbecoming as a follower of Him. I cannot serve

God fully with things that are displeasing to Him. That is why the Lord shows us things that we need to change or just get rid of. This can be a very hard process because sometimes we don't want to let go of a hurt and forgive someone. Sometimes we don't want to think nice thoughts about a mean and nasty person much less pray for them to receive blessings!

Even though your hurt feelings may be justified and God knows that a certain person is not nice, our Lord Jesus loves them anyway. When I think about it that way, I feel ashamed. How can God give us the underserved *love* that He wants to give if we can't love others who are underserving as well?

We cannot go further and deepen our relationship with God unless we fully surrender our lives in all areas. Our loving God desires to give us His fullness and riches in overwhelming quantities. In Isaiah 45:3, God tells us this: "I will give you hidden treasures, riches stored in secret places, so that you may know that I am the Lord, the God of Israel, who summons you by name." I can just see the heavenly Father standing before me with treasures stacked up all around Him. All of these treasures have my name on them. Some of them are dusty and have been sitting there for a while. Those are the ones that I have refused to open. Priceless treasures unopened and wasted because of my stubbornness, laziness, fear, hatred, doubt, and pride. How sad that must make my heavenly Father for His child to so blindly refuse His gifts.

In your daily walk with God, look and listen and see what He brings to the surface like the buckled floor. Are there things that need to change or that you need to rid yourself of? What remains in those hidden places? Listen to the sweet Holy Spirit and receive God's gifts instead of sending them back.

In 2 Corinthians 4:7–8, Paul states, "But we have this treasure in jars of clay to show that this all-surpassing power is from God and not from us. We are hard pressed on every side, but not crushed; perplexed, but not in despair; persecuted, but not abandoned; struck down, but not destroyed." We are rich in *love* from God himself. As our dear Lord's living water flows within us, I pray that we all listen, purge, and receive. When I stand before the Lord, I don't want to see a stack of unopened and wasted gifts at His feet. I want to see only His glory and His open arms welcoming me home!

The Multiplying Inheritance

he young man looked at the flyer. It stated that the old man's funeral would be at two that afternoon. It also stated that the man had a very large inheritance that his children would be sharing with anyone who attended the service. You did not have to be a friend of the old man or even an acquaintance.

The young father of two tied his shoes and put on his only tie. He went downstairs to find his wife reading a story to his two little ones. He could hear her telling about a man named Daniel being thrown into the lion's den. The children gasped, and the little girl covered her ears.

The boy asked if Daniel was eaten up. "No," said his mother. "The Lord was with him, and He shut the lion's mouths. Not one hair was touched on Daniel's head, and none of his clothes were torn. God delivered Daniel from the lion's den without one single scratch."

"Daddy," the little boy said, "do you believe that story is true?"

"Well, it must be, son," said his father. "It is the Bible after all."

The man did believe in God, and Jesus was his Savior. Although, he didn't make it to church very often, his wife, on the other hand, did attend church regularly, and she was always reading stories to the children from the Bible. She often told them how much God loves them and how he gave us His Son Jesus to save them.

The man put on his hat and told his family that he would be back in a while. His wife could see that he was holding the folded flyer in his hand. She asked him if he was going to the old man's funeral. He told her yes. The man was hoping that he could cash in on some free inheritance. Times had been hard for the little family. The father just barely made it month to month with the bills. The mother did alterations for people to try and help bring in extra money. It would be good for them to have a little breathing room for a change.

He kissed them all good-bye and left the house. The church was a few blocks away. He took off walking in that direction. When he arrived, there was a crowd of people already filing inside to see if they might have a chance as well at this mysterious inheritance. The man got in line and was soon sitting in a pew with the rest of the crowd.

There was a simple casket in the front of the church. It was adorned with flowers that came from the gardens at the church. You see, the old man was the caretaker and the gardener there. He had worked there for many years. The outside of the church ways always immaculate and beautifully landscaped. The inside was as clean as a whistle as well.

The young man could see what appeared to be the old man's family. They walked down the aisle and were seated at the front. They weren't from around there. His son and daughter had moved away long ago. They were both married now and had children of their own.

The piano music played softly in the background. Soon an elderly lady came and stood at the microphone. She sang about God's eye being on the sparrow and watching over her. She sang let not your heart be troubled and that she was happy and free.

Next, the pastor came to address the crowd. He welcomed them all. He motioned for the ushers in the back to come forward. They were all carrying large baskets filled with something rectangular shaped. They were all wrapped in simple brown paper. Everyone in the church was given a package. The pastor said that was part of the inheritance that was spoken about on the flyer. He instructed them not to open the packages until they were at home.

The young man's mind was racing. It felt like a book. Maybe the man was a famous author, and he had been writing under an anonymous name all these years. Maybe the book's pages were filled with hundred-dollar bills! The possibilities were endless. What if some of the packages had more money than the others? What if there was a single check in his package for a million dollars? The brown paper burned in his hands as he played out the different scenarios in his mind.

The pastor introduced the old man's son and told the crowd that he would be explaining about another part of the old man's inheritance. The old man's son came to the microphone. He had a friendly smile on his face. He did not look sad at all. The young man found this to be a little bit strange.

As the son spoke, he recalled many happy memories that he and his sister had of their father. He explained that their father was a simple man. He stated that their upbringing was modest, and they never had much, but they always had enough. He surprised the crowd by saying that his father may have been one of the richest men in the county. He said that his wealth was so vast that they decided to share it with others. He said that they had been enjoying the fortune handed down to them from their father for many years. He stated that the more they shared their wealth, the more it kept multiplying and spreading in all directions to all kinds of people. You see, the son confessed this inheritance never runs out! It just keeps building.

The young man was completely baffled by now. Had the old man found a hidden treasure in his youth? Was he really a secret heir to a dynasty? What were they all about to receive?

The son continued his explanation. "My father is an heir to a king."

The young man's heart skipped a beat. He knew it! The old man was royalty! The son went on to say that he himself was a prince, and his sister was a princess. Their king was very powerful and wise. He resided in beauty and splendor. He was loving and true. The son's eyes studied the crowd. "You see, he said God Almighty is the King of whom I speak of. My father is his child. During his time, here on earth he lived as a child of God. He was rich beyond measure. In turn he made sure that my sister and I knew all about God. He and our mother taught us everything about our heavenly Father and our heritage as believers. He made sure to leave us a heritage of faith and knowledge.

"Our father worked hard while he lived on this earth. Like I said, we never had much material wise, but we always had enough. However, my father's spiritual wealth was incredible. He had a simple and humble faith. He loved to tell others about God and His love for us through Jesus Christ. My father taught us how to store up our riches in heaven where moth and rust cannot destroy. He modeled how we are to share those riches with others here on earth.

"By the time my sister and I were ready to leave home, our father had willed his entire fortune over to us. We were set for life, so to speak. My sister and I would like to share this vast fortune with all of you here today. If you are a believer in Christ, then you are already an heir yourself. I urge you as his child to use his fortune wisely throughout your lives. Don't waste it by neglecting to share it with others. If you are not a believer, we urge you to accept God's free gift of salvation and become an heir to the King. You will be rich beyond measure! As you, in turn, share this inheritance, you will be amazed as you watch it multiply before your eyes!

"Most importantly, always make it a point to share this glorious inheritance with your children. You are to speak of it day and night." Then he read a passage from his Bible to the crowd, "Start children off on the way they should go, and even when they are old they will not turn from it, Proverb 22:6."

The man went on to say that the item in the brown package is just what everyone needs to do that. He told them that it was his father's idea. He explained how his father had handwritten a note before he went home to the Lord. He had instructed his son and daughter to make copies and place them along with the other item inside the package. His hope was that all of the people attending the service would become even richer and would pass the wealth on to be multiplied. The son thanked everyone for their time, and the crowd was dismissed.

The young man stayed seated in the pew. Some people were angry as they got up to leave. He heard people whisper under their breath that this was stupid. Some people were excited, and some were like the young man, slightly dazed and in deep thought. He gathered his hat and the brown package and started home.

It was a beautiful spring afternoon, although the young man could see rain clouds billowing up in the distance. Thunderstorms were predicted for that evening. As he walked in the direction of home, he could smell the rain already in the air. He could hear thunder off in the distance. The birds were still singing and flying about even though the storm was approaching. They didn't seem to have a care in the world.

His eye is on the sparrow, came into his thoughts. *If His eye is on the sparrow, then it must surely be on me*, he reminded himself. *Life's storms will come and go*, he thought, *but God's Son Jesus is always shining through them all. His eye is always on me, and His mighty hand will never let me fall.*

He turned the door handle and opened the door. There before him sat a princess sewing someone else's clothes. Her own were worn but clean and pressed. She smiled as he came and kissed her cheek. He sat the brown package on her lap.

"What is this?" she asked.

"That is your inheritance," he said. "Everyone at the service received one. We were instructed not to

open them until we returned home. I'm giving you the honors."

She carefully opened the package. It was a simple black Bible. Inside it was a white piece of paper folded in half. It was the note from the old man. It said, "Dear friend, I'm glad that you came and received your inheritance today. Just always remember to keep using it and to share it with others. That is the only way it will multiply!" It was signed, "Your friend, Ben."

"A Bible," the young man said, "I should have known."

"What a kind gesture," his wife said. She thumbed through its pages, and a check fell out on the floor.

When she picked it up, she could see that it was written out to Smith's Mercantile for $34.97. Smith's was an old family store in town. They carried everything from hardware to groceries to fabric.

"Oh, dear," she said, "this must have been placed in the Bible by mistake." It was dated a few days before the old man's death and signed by him.

She got up immediately and called the store. She told them that she had found the old man's check in the Bible that her husband had received at the service. She said that she would bring it to them first thing the next morning.

The man at the store laughed and said, "Oh no, ma'am, that check is for you. Old Ben called us a few days before he passed and told us that people would be bringing us these checks. We were told that you would be needing something specific from our store and that the check would cover it."

The young wife hung up the phone. She had a puzzled look on her face. She walked over to her purse and dug out a scrap piece of paper. She had written down a price of something at Smith's on that paper. She opened it up and burst into tears. It said $34.97. Her husband asked her what was wrong. She showed him the piece of paper and told him how it was the exact amount of the check. She told him what the man on the phone had told her. She explained that she had been saving money for them all to have new clothes for Easter. She bought a dress for her daughter and a new shirt and tie for her son. She even bought her husband a new shirt and tie as a surprise. That took all of the money she had saved. She found a beautiful periwinkle-blue dress for her, but with tax it was going to be $34.97. She had not told anyone about the dress, not even God.

The man sat there in awe of this Almighty God. "His eye is on the sparrow," he said, with a lump in his throat. "That's the song that was sung at the old man's funeral service today."

"Yes," she said, "that's in the Bible. In Matthew 10:29–31, Jesus tell his disciples, 'Are not two sparrows sold for a penny? Yet not one of them will fall to the ground outside your Father's care. And even the very hairs of your head are all numbered. So, don't be afraid; you are worth more than many sparrows.'"

"We don't have a lot," the young man said, "but we have enough. Thank you, God! Help me, Lord, to receive your beautiful inheritance every day. Show me how to share it with my family and friends so that it can multiply and spread to others. Forgive me for not showing my children your way. Help me to speak about you to them always. In Jesus's name, amen."

"Amen," said his wife.

That Easter was a special one for the little family. They celebrated and thanked God for sending His one and only Son Jesus to die for their sins. They praised God for raising Him from the dead and placing Him on the throne.

The family of four walked home from church that day hand in hand. All of them were wearing their new Easter attire. The young man noticed how stunning his wife looked in her new periwinkle-blue dress. God's eye was on his family; he knew that full well. He smiled and thanked the Lord for this sweet Easter blessing. It was one of many to come, since he was rich with inheritance from a King!

> Give joyful thanks to the Father, who has qualified you to share in the inheritance of His holy people in the kingdom of light. (Col 1:12)

> My goal is that they may be encouraged in heart and united in love, so that they may have the full riches of complete understanding, in order that they may know the mystery of God, namely, Christ, in whom are hidden all the treasures of wisdom and knowledge. (Col 2:2–3)

THE
WEA
TRAVELER

By Andi

The Weary Traveler

a man approached me one day and asked this question: "Excuse me, but can you tell me how to get to no. 1 Forgiveness Way? I hear that there is a very nice house there and that the owner welcomes all sorts of people. It's said that He gives free room and board. And just by receiving the free gift that He offers, you can stay there for eternity! I also heard that when you live there, you are never sick, tired, sad, or scared. The owner's Son takes care of you, and He offers true friendship and wants to share all of His riches with everyone. I've been driving around for a very long while. So far everyone that I've asked can't tell me where the house is or the owner's name, much less His Son's name. Do you by any chance know where I can find no. 1 Forgiveness Way? I have almost lost all hope that it even exists!"

I looked at the man with his questioning eyes and tired expression. I smiled at him, and I said, "Of course, I know directions to that house! I have a lovely room reserved for me there. It's not ready yet, but the Son is working on it. He is adding new things for me there all the time. He knows everything that I need. I'm certain you will love it there! Except you need to hurry and accept the owner's free gift right away. The offer won't stand forever. In time He will know when no one else wants His gift and close His doors. You don't want to miss this once-in-a-lifetime opportunity!"

The man enthusiastically said, "I'm in! Just tell me what to do."

So, I started explaining to him about how to get his own free room at no. 1 Forgiveness Way. I asked him, "Do you believe in God?"

The man answered, "Yes, I do believe there is a God somewhere."

I explained to him that God has a Son named Jesus who has been with Him always. Together with the Holy Spirit they formed the universe and everything in it. God made man and woman in His image. They chose to sin against God. That is why we live in a fallen world today. We needed a sacrifice for our sins. God loves us so much that He sent His only Son

Jesus to die for our sins on the cross so that we could be forgiven. God's forgiveness allows us to spend eternity with Him in His beautiful heavenly home.

I showed him my Bible, and I told him that it is a book that is written by God through men that He chose. I read to him that he was fearfully and wonderfully made, Psalm 139:14. I also read to him John 3:16: "For God so loved the world that He gave His one and only Son, that whoever believes in Him shall not perish but have eternal life."

In John 14:2–4, I shared with him that Jesus says, "In my Father's house are many rooms. I am going there to prepare a place for you. I will come back and take you to be with me that you also may be where I am. You know the way to the place where I am going."

The man just stood there before me with his mouth opened wide. With a single tear sliding down his cheek, he asked, "Why? Why would God let His only Son die for me? Why would they offer me their home for free?"

I explained to the man that God created him and that he knew everything about him, and he loved him very much. He had to send Jesus to bridge the gap that sin had made between us. He is our bridge so to speak that enables us to reach God.

The man then asked me, "So where does this free gift come in?"

I told him, "Oh, that's as easy as 123. First, *admit* that you are a sinner. We are all sinners and need forgiveness. All you have to do is ask for forgiveness and turn away from your sin" (Rom 6:23).

"Second, *believe* that Jesus is God's Son and that God sent Him to save us all from our sins. Jesus died on the cross and rose from the dead" (Rom 5:8).

"Third, *confess* that you want Jesus to be Lord of your life and commit your life to Him. Trust Jesus to be your Lord and Savior" (Rom 10:13).

The man bowed his head, and I led him in the prayer of salvation. When we finished, he smiled as many tears ran down his cheeks, and he said, "Now I have a permanent reservation with God. He will never leave me. The Holy Spirit will always be my helper. Jesus will always be speaking on my behalf."

He thanked me and turned, making a beeline for his car. I asked him where he was going in such a rush.

He answered with urgency in his voice, "Well, I have friends and family that I need to tell how to make a reservation! And who knows, I might encounter weary strangers along the way who are looking for directions to no. 1 Forgiveness Way! I have good news to tell before God's offer expires."

As he opened his car door, he waved and said, "I'll see you at the house sometime."

I smiled and said, "Okay, I'll be looking for you, friend."

As I waved good-bye, I said a prayer for my new friend in Christ. I also thanked our sweet Lord for my reserved room in heaven. As I turned to go inside, I looked and saw another car coming down the road, and I thought to myself, *I wonder whose house that person is looking for? I hope that they have found God and they have their reservation."*

Jesus tells us this: "Come to me all you who are weary and burdened, and I will give you rest" (Matt 11:28).

SOLAR LIGHTS

I have had this one solar yard light for over a year. I bought it to try out and see if I might want to put them in my yard. It has sat in different places in my house. At the present time, it's next to my back door. Every time that I walk by it, I say to myself that I really need to put that out somewhere and let it charge.

As I walked by the solar light the other day, I thought about how we as Christians live our lives like the solar yard light. We have the ability and the responsibility to be lights to the world. The problem is we never make time to get charged by the Son.

In Psalm 36:9, the psalmist tells us this about God: "For with You is the fountain of life; in your light we see light." We don't realize how badly we need this charging through daily prayer filled with praise, thanksgiving, requests, and confessing along with the reading of God's word. It seems that sons and daughters of God go through life ill-equipped to handle turmoil. Without our daily charge, how can we expect to handle life's struggles, much less be a light for others who so desperately need us! Jesus tells us in John 8:12, "I am the light of the world. Whoever follows me will never walk in darkness, but will have the light of life."

A lot of Christians get *charged* on Sundays only. That isn't enough to get you through the week. Some Christians charge only in times of crisis. Many Christians stay in the infant stage of their walk with God because after they accept Christ as their Savior, they aren't shown the importance of daily fellowship with God. A lot of us live life defeated because we just don't realize the importance of this daily blessing and the strength that comes from being in God's presence.

What we don't understand is that God is waiting for each of us every day to fellowship with us. Before we open our eyes, He is telling us, "Good morning, sunshine! I love you so. Won't you sit and talk with me for a while?"

In 2 Chronicles 16:9, scripture tells us, "For the eyes of the Lord range throughout the earth to strengthen those whose hearts are fully committed to Him." He looks for us and waits for us!

In Proverbs 8:17, God tells us, "I love those who love me, and those who seek me find me." God loves us with such fury and power, but most of the time we fail to embrace Him. He sits by wanting to help, but we, to no avail, keep trying to do it all by ourselves. Deuteronomy 33:26 tells us that "there is no one like the God of Israel who rides on the heavens to help you and on the clouds in His majesty." Why do we try to do everything with our own strength when we have a mighty God ready to help?

Jesus, God's Son, gives us very specific instructions. In Matthew 5:14, He says, "You are a light of the world. A city on a hill cannot be hidden." In Matthew 5:16, He tells us to "Let your light shine before men, that they may see your good deeds and praise your Father in heaven."

If we are not getting *charged*, how can our light shine? We have to be receiving God's light in order to shine His light. Ephesians 5:8 says, "For you were once darkness, but now you are light in the Lord. Live as children of light for the fruit of light consists in all goodness, righteousness and truth and find out what pleases the Lord."

We as Christians are God's children and lights of hope. When I think about that, I see God looking down on this darkened world and seeing His children lighting the way. Have you ever been on an airplane at night? You look out the window, and you see darkness. Soon you fly over a city, and you are greeted by the warm glow of the twinkling lights. I think God sees us that way.

As we shine our lights for others, we call out to them into the darkness and say, "It's okay, God loves you! Step out of the dark and into the Son's light!" I know that God is pleased when His little lights shine.

Dear brothers and sisters, please take time and *charge* your lights! People need God. We as God's children shine the way to our Lord Jesus Christ. Don't just leave your soul lying around in the dark. We need the life-giving power of the Son in our lives every day. In 1John 3:1, scripture says, "How great is the love the Father has lavished on us, that we should be called children of God! And that is what we are!"

So, children of God, I give you this challenge. Pick up your light, get charged, and shine! You will be blessed, and the world will see your light in the darkness shining the way to our *almighty God* and eternal life.

The MAN with the broken heart

Andi

THE MAN WITH THE
BROKEN HEART

The elderly man had received some unsettling news. He had an irregular heartbeat and would have to receive a pacemaker to correct the problem. As he left the doctor's office, a weight of anxiety settled on him. The doctor told him that it would be a simple procedure, and it was quite common among elderly folks like himself.

When he returned home from his doctor's visit, he sat down in his comfy chair and sipped his cup of coffee. As he leaned his head back, his eyes felt heavy. Before he knew it, he was fast asleep. His wife covered him up with a blanket and let him rest.

Soon the sound of the alarm clock woke him with a start. He could hear his wife saying, "Hurry, dear, you need to get ready. Today you will get your pacemaker."

He thought to himself that he must have been very tired. He couldn't even remember going to bed last night. He got up and began to get himself ready. Soon they were headed for the hospital.

When he arrived, he was given papers to sign and a bracelet to wear. They took him to his room where he was to wait. Nurses came in and asked him questions and filled out more papers. They hooked him up with all kinds of wires and poked him with needles.

A bright-eyed nurse came in and said that she needed to ask him some questions. The first question she asked was if he believed in God.

He looked at his wife and shrugged his shoulders, saying, "Well, I guess so."

Next, she asked if he believed that his Son was Jesus Christ. He looked at his wife again wondering if she had brought him to a special church hospital or something.

He said, "Well, I've heard that story, but I really haven't thought much about it."

"Hmm, so have you ever felt the need to ask Jesus to be your personal Savior and make your heart new?" the nurse asked.

He said, "Well, my wife here does all of that Jesus stuff, but I don't. When Sunday morning gets here, I'm either resting from the workweek or catching up on other things." He looked at the nurse and said, "If you don't mind me asking, why do you need to know all of these answers just to give me a pacemaker?"

"A pacemaker," the nurse said. She flipped through her papers and looked at them carefully. She looked at the man very seriously and said, "Sir, I have a diagnosis here and treatment, but it's not for a pacemaker."

The man sat up in the bed and asked, "Then what am I here for?"

The nurse told him, "Sir, you have a broken heart."

"I know," said the man. "That's why I'm here for a pacemaker!"

"Umm, no, sir," she said, "you won't be getting a pacemaker today."

The man could feel his heart inside his chest as it seemed to be doing somersaults. He closed his eyes trying to stay calm and said, "So exactly what am I here for today?"

The nurse gently touched his arm and said, "You are here for a new heart."

"You mean I'm getting a heart transplant?" the man asked in alarm.

"In a way, yes," said the nurse. "Now lay back and relax. The surgical team will be in to get you soon."

The man looked at his wife, and she smiled at him. She told him that everything would be just fine. She said that lots of people get new hearts all the time. She laughed and told him how all of them wished that they would have done it years earlier after receiving their new hearts.

The man folded his arms in protest and said, "Well, that's not what I'm here for today. Someone has made a mistake. I'm here for a pacemaker, not a new heart! I won't do it."

"Okay," said his wife. "It's your choice, not mine."

About that time the nurse came in, and he told her that he would like to go home because he didn't want a new heart today. She looked at him sadly and said, "Awe, I'm sorry, sir. If that's what you really want, then I'll start the paperwork for your release."

"I'm completely sure," the man said.

The nurse made a few notes, and she left the room.

Soon a tall and muscular male attendant came in the room. He was wearing scrubs and a lab coat. He explained that he was from the discharge department. "Good morning, sir," he said. "I understand that you are refusing the new heart and that you prefer to keep your broken one. Is that correct?"

"Yes it is," the old man said sharply.

"Okay, just let me finish this paperwork, and you will be on your way," said the attendant.

"Okay, the number one reason for release is that the patient has Psalm 17:10 disease, which makes him a difficult candidate for a new heart."

"Wait a minute," the old man said. "What is Psalm 17:10 disease?"

"Oh, that, sir, reads as follows," the man said. He looked at his sheet and read off the meaning of Psalm 17:10 disease, "It says here that you have closed your unfeeling heart, and with your mouth you speak proudly," stated the attendant.

"Well, I never," said the old man. "I have done nothing of the sort! I came in here and answered a few questions, and the next thing I knew, you were giving me a whole new heart instead of a pacemaker!"

The attendant reminded the old man that he did state that he never really thought about Jesus being God's Son and that he didn't mess with that Jesus stuff and church, but his wife did.

"Yes," the old man said, "that is true."

"So," said the attendant, "therefore you suffer from Psalm 17:10 disease."

"Okay," the old man said, rolling his eyes. "If that gets me out of here, then so be it. Psalm 17:10 disease it is!"

"All righty then," said the attendant. "The number two reason for release is that the patient realizes that the disease is curable but still refuses the healing treatment. If I can just get you to initial here, sir, we can move on to number three."

"Okay," said the old man, "you know that I have to ask what is this treatment that I am refusing to take."

"Oh, that's a simple and painless treatment. Although some people chose to die rather than accept it. It's called the Romans 10:9–13 cure. The treatment is as follows: 'For whoever calls on the name of the Lord shall be saved. If you confess with your mouth the Lord Jesus and believe in your heart that God has raised Him from the dead, you will be saved. For with the heart one believes unto righteousness and with the mouth confession is made unto salvation.'

"Following this treatment, the Ezekiel 36:26 process begins, which is as follows: 'Moreover, I will give you a new heart and put a new spirit within you; and I will remove the heart of stone from your flesh and give you a heart of flesh.'"

The man put his initial next to statement number two.

"Now," said the attendant, "on to our third and final statement for release. Patient is fully aware and understands the consequences of living with a broken heart rather than accepting a new one. Please initial here."

The old man initialed and asked, "So what are the consequences of a broken heart?"

The attendant looked solemnly at the old man and said, "'Everyone who acknowledges Christ on earth He will also acknowledge before the Father in heaven. But, everyone who denies Christ here on earth, He will also deny before His Father in heaven. That's from Matthew 10:31–33."

"Jesus also said in Luke 12:9 that 'anyone who denies me here on earth will be denied before God's angels.' You see," said the attendant, "when you acknowledge that Jesus Christ is God's Son and the Savior of the world, your sins are forgiven, and your heart is made new. The old and broken heart is replaced by a new one. You are able to receive joy and peace through God's grace. The Holy Spirit helps you and guides you. He never leaves your side."

The attendant excused himself and said someone would be in shortly to take him downstairs so that he could return home. The old man laid his head back on the pillow and closed his eyes. He thought to himself, *Wow, what a mixed up and stressful morning this has been!*

Suddenly he felt a soft tapping on his shoulder and heard his wife saying, "Wake up, honey, it's time for dinner."

The old man opened his eyes and saw his wife's smiling face. He said, "How did I get home from the hospital?"

She laughed and said, "You have been sleeping all afternoon. You must have been having some dream because you tossed and mumbled for quite a while. Your appointment at the hospital isn't until tomorrow."

"You mean all of this was just a dream?" the man asked. "I'm not going to have a heart transplant?"

His wife chuckled and said, "Well, I hope not! I think it will just be a pacemaker tomorrow."

He leaned back and thought about the strange dream. He looked at his wife and said, "Honey, do you think that I have a broken heart?"

She looked at him thoughtfully and said, "What exactly do you mean?"

"Well," he said, "in my dream that's why I needed a heart transplant because mine was broken. They told me that I had Psalm 17:10 disease but that it could be cured by the Romans 10:9–13 treatment. They said that my heart was hard because I didn't acknowledge Jesus as God's Son, and therefore I didn't ask Him to be my Savior so that He could give me a new heart."

"Well, honey, Jesus is the only way to have true peace and joy in this life here on earth. He is our saving grace. Through Him we have eternal life. If we do not acknowledge Christ here on earth then, He won't acknowledge us in heaven before the Father," said his wife.

"That's what the attendant told me in the dream," said the man.

The old man and his wife sat quietly that evening as they ate their dinner. The man kept mulling the dream over and over in his mind.

When they went to bed, he lay there in the dark, still thinking about his dream. He felt the soft touch of his wife's hand on his cheek. He heard her as she softly whispered a prayer over her husband.

"Dear Lord," she said, "please watch over this sweet man tomorrow. Help him to know God, how special he is to you, and how much you love him. Help him to see the importance of knowing Jesus as his Savior and Lord. Give him a restful sleep tonight and bless him, Lord. I ask these things in the name of Jesus. Amen." She kissed him good night and was soon asleep herself snoring softly.

His eyes opened to the ringing of the alarm clock.

"Six o'clock." He heard his wife say. "Time to get up."

He sat up on the edge of the bed. He knew what he had to do. He called to his wife, and she came and stood by his side asking him what he needed. The old man said, "Honey, I don't want to have a broken heart anymore. I want Jesus to give me a new one."

His wife smiled as a tear slid down her cheek. "Okay" she said, "would you like me to pray with you?"

"Yes," he said as he bowed his head. He softly began to speak. "Jesus," he said, "I do recognize you as God's Son. I do believe that you died for my sins so that I can be made new. I confess my sins to you,

Lord, and I ask that you will forgive me. Please, Jesus, be my Savior today and always. Come and be Lord of my life. Amen."

He felt a sudden relief and gladness in his heart. He laughed to himself as he wondered why he hadn't done this years ago. His wife hugged him and kissed his tears as she wiped her own.

They got ready and headed to the hospital. When they arrived, it was a lot like his dream. Papers to fill out, wires being hooked to him, and needles that poked.

A bright-eyed nurse came into the room. She told him that she had some questions for him. He smiled and said, "Ask away."

She stated that he would be having a pacemaker today and asked if that was correct. He said yes and giggled a little. She stated that he certainly was in good spirits and asked him if he was always this happy.

He said, "Well, now the old me could be pretty cranky at times, but the new me is different. You see, I already had a heart procedure this morning. I had a new heart given to me by my Savior Jesus Christ. Mine was broken, so I asked Him to give me a new one, and He did! Now, I am able to have peace and joy even in the hard times. Even when I'm in need of a pacemaker."

"Well now, that's the best news that I've heard today," the nurse said with a smile. "Only Jesus can fix a broken heart, you know. We keep them beating here at the hospital, but God, the true Physician, mends the ones that are cracked." She left the room closing the door behind her.

The old man reached for his wife's hand and said, "Thank you for never giving up on me." He closed his eyes and said, "Thank you, Lord, for never giving up on me either. Thank you for healing this foolish man's heart and making it new."

> The Lord is not slow in keeping His promise as some understand slowness. Instead He is patient with you, not wanting anyone to perish, but everyone to come to repentance. (2 Pet 3:9)

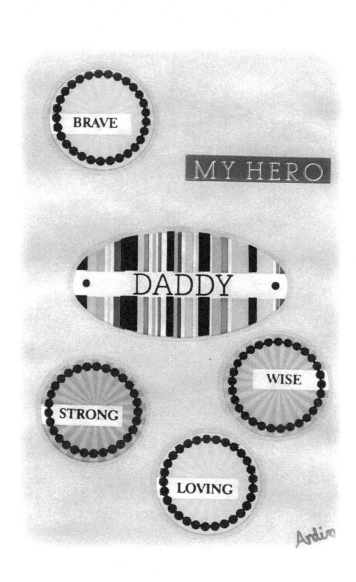

DADDY

A friend of mine once shared with me about his experience of caring for a foster child and later adopting him as his son. As I listened to his story, I couldn't help seeing a connection with the heavenly Father and His children.

The story starts out with a young toddler who had been abused, neglected, and starved. He was left in a cold, dark basement for long periods of time to grope around for food. He was also made to live in a parked car outside his own home. When he came to live with my friend, he was scared and in great need of love and affection.

My friend said that the first time he met his son, there was a fence between them. My friend stuck his finger through the fence and said hello. The boy immediately grabbed my friend's finger and said the word *daddy*. When they had to appear in court with the biological parents, the small boy would hold on to my friend's neck so tight that it choked him because he was terrified that he would be sent back with them. I told my friend that because of his willingness to share his home and his love with this child, he had saved the boy's life.

That's how it is with our heavenly Father. He is so willing to share His love and His home with all of us. We a lot of times have other ideas. We go through this life abused. We oftentimes abuse ourselves or others. By neglecting to see the love of God, we go through life feeling neglected. God's love for us is powerful and life changing.

In John 3:16, Jesus says, "For God so loved the world that He gave His one and only Son, that whoever believes in Him shall not perish but have eternal life."

In Romans 5:8, scripture tells us this: "But God demonstrates His own love for us in this: While we were still sinners, Christ died for us."

We may be fed with worldly things, but we are wasting away inside because we are starving spiritually. God longs to feed us and make us strong. In Psalm 107:9, it says that He satisfies the thirsty and fills the hungry with good things.

As humans, we grope around in the dark, when all along the light is right in front of us. We know that we need something, but we can't find it. Scripture tells us in Isaiah 9:2 that the people walking in darkness have seen a great light; a light has dawned on those living in the land of darkness. Jesus is that great light! Jesus tells us in John 8:12, "I am the light of the world. Whoever follows me will never walk in darkness, but will have the light of life."

We need unfailing love and affection, but there is a fence in our way. God is on the other side of the fence, but Jesus is waiting by the gate! He calls our name and offers His hand for us to take. All you have to do is decide to walk through it and take Jesus by the hand. Our heavenly Father longs to hear our voice call Him by name. He waits for us to throw our arms around His love, never wanting to let go of Him and clinging to Him to keep from returning to the old life. God longs to bless us and save our lives. He longs to share His love and ultimately His eternal home. We just have to be willing to stop looking through the fence and walk through the gate.

However, people are always afraid that they will have to give up too much if they make that choice. They want to be free and make all of the decisions themselves. What they don't realize is that when you accept Christ to be Lord and Savior of your life, you are letting Him set you free. Galatians 5:1 tells us it is for freedom that Christ has set us free. Stand firm then and do not let yourselves be burdened again by a yoke of slavery.

In 2 Corinthians 3:17, scripture says, "Now the Lord is the Spirit, and where the Spirit of the Lord is, there is freedom." As you know, true freedom always comes at a price. The great news is that debt has already been paid in full when Jesus died for us on the cross. By doing so, the gate was flung open wide for all to enter by just saying yes to His gift of life. It's so easy yet so hard for some to do.

We all were or still are that small child looking for someone to take care of us. We need only look to God and His Son Jesus Christ for that care. These verses say it all in Romans 3:22–24: "This righteousness from God comes through faith in Jesus Christ to all who believe. There is no difference, for all have sinned and fall short of the glory of God, and are justified freely by His grace through the redemption that came by Christ Jesus."

I give thanks to my friend for rescuing this sweet young man that I know today. God knew that the scared little boy would be in good hands with the kind man he called Daddy. Just like my friend, God is waiting to hear us all say His name.

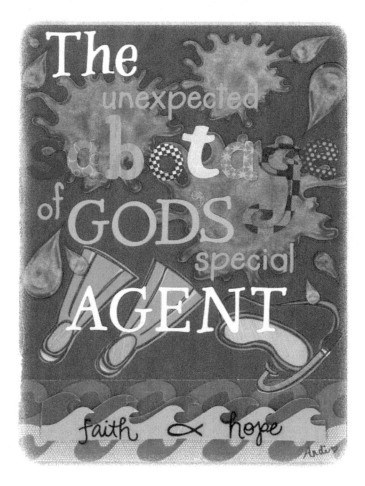

The
unexpected
sabotage
of GODS
special
AGENT

faith & hope

Andi

The Unexpected Sabotage
of God's Special Agent

The young woman was awakened by a dream early one morning. In the dream, she could see herself in a dark and dangerous place. She was on a very important mission right in the middle of enemy territory. Someone with great authority and power had sent her to do this task. At one point, she was to dive deep down into the dark and uncharted water. She had been on these missions before, but never one like this one. It was different.

This one was more difficult. The woman was having trouble seeing where she was going. She was deep in the middle of her mission when she felt a touch on her shoulder. She spun around and came face-to-face with the enemy. He was dressed all in black. She knew him. She had dealt with him many times before. The man took her by the arm and she began to cry. She was crippled by the power of his presence. He took her in his arms and she sobbed as he held her. He held her not in a consoling and loving way, but as his victim with destruction in his heart.

As he led her away she knew that she would slowly die if she did not fight back. Yet, she remained there frozen, almost in a trance as he led her to his prison.

When the woman awoke from her nightmarish dream she was both puzzled and bothered. She thought about it for several days. She asked the Lord to help her to understand what the dream meant.

From as far back as she could remember she had been plagued by the spirit of fear. As a little girl, she slept with the light on. She would hear noises at night outside her bedroom window. Her imagination would run wild and many nights she ended up in her parents' bed where she felt safe. She still lived in fear as an adult. The fear of failing. The fear of being laughed at. The fear of not being accepted. The fear of what if…

In the Bible, we are told hundreds of times not to fear. Jesus tells us in John 14:27, "Peace I leave with you; my peace I give you. I do not give to you as the world gives. Do not let your hearts be troubled and do not be afraid."

Days passed as she pondered if there was anything significant about the important mission, the man in black, the deepness of the water and the difficulty seeing. She also wondered why she just gave up and started crying, aborting her mission completely at the single touch of the mysterious man in black.

The man—He was obviously someone whom she had dealt with before. What was his stronghold over her? Why didn't she even fight back? As she applied the dream to some of the things that were going on in her own life, the two seemed to be running parallel.

She saw herself on a very important and special mission. She had been entrusted by God himself to live out this mission. She was responsible for living out her life as an example for others. As a follower of Jesus, she was expected to pray continually for fellow brothers and sisters in Christ as well as the unsaved.

Her mission in life was clear. She along with all followers of Jesus Christ was to share the gospel of truth during her time here on earth. In Mark 16:15 Jesus tells us to "go into the world and preach the gospel to all creation."

The woman knew that she wouldn't have to travel far. There were plenty of people in her small town who needed to hear some good news. She was to live this one life that she had been given with joy and peace, even in the rough times.

The man in black. She saw him being the enemy, Satan. Whenever she prayed for those lost souls or lived out her mission by doing God's will, he was right there. He knew her well. He knew her strengths and weaknesses. He knew how to make her afraid, how to make her cry and give up. He had nothing but hate and darkness in his heart for her and all of mankind.

He especially hated followers of Jesus. Satan waits to sift us all like wheat just as he did Simon (Peter) in Luke 22. But Jesus prayed for him as He prays for us and intercedes every day, every hour, every minute, on our behalf! "Therefore He is able to save completely those who come to God through Him, because He always lives to intercede for them" (Heb 7:25).

As she reflected once again on her dream, she noted that the enemy didn't use force. He didn't have a weapon to hold her against her will. All he used was manipulation and the lie of greater power. She could have overpowered him at any time. God had

given her all she needed for her fight. He would not send anyone out on a special mission without their necessary armor.

The deep and murky water was her next thought. In her dream, she had not gone down into that deep of water before. As we grow in our walk with the Lord, He does take us deeper. Sometimes the deeper we go the more difficult it gets. If we are praying for the lost and witnessing to them, the enemy won't like that. Those are his people and he won't give them up without a fight. In other words, he will be tapping on your shoulder soon. Be ready for his lies and scare tactics. 1 Peter 5:8 says, "Be alert and of sober mind. Your enemy the devil prowls around like a roaring lion looking for someone to devour."

Although the woman was told to go deeper, she was protected. She had a mask and an air tank in her dream. She even had a light for the deepest and darkest parts. Some areas however were not only dark but murky too. In those areas, she had to trust and look for the light. When God takes us deeper, He does protect us. He sustains us with His life saving power. He lights our way. Although we can't always see what He is doing on this end, He is already at work shedding light on the other end!

"Even in darkness light dawns for the upright, for the gracious and compassionate and righteous man and woman" (Ps 112:4).

Everything came together about the dream. The woman realized that she was on an ongoing mission for the Lord. She was many things to Him. She was an entrusted ambassador, a witness, a warrior, a beautiful scent that fills this world and a cherished daughter of the Most High God! He had called her and she had answered.

"My heart says of You, 'Seek His face!' Your face, Lord I will seek" (Ps 27:8). He trusted her with the lives of others. He depended on her loving words and actions to change lives. He spoke to her discerning spirit to know when to speak and when to listen. He heard her prayers for others and prayers for herself. He moved in and through her. She was an open vessel longing to be used by God himself to bring Him glory. God's glory shines through when others recognize Jesus as Lord.

2 Corinthians 4:6 says, "For God, who said, 'Let light shine out of darkness,' made His light shine in our hearts to give us the light of the knowledge of God's glory displayed in the face of Christ." God's glory shines when strangers are helped or loved ones are encouraged. It shines as we comfort and pray for

others. She had been doing a lot of those things not even realizing what an impact she was having for God's kingdom.

As God took her deeper the enemy attacked harder. For a time, the waters had been deep, dark, murky, and even very scary. She would often cry and feel defeated. Little did she know that Satan was behind it all. He knew that she was destined to do great things for God's kingdom. All of God's children are destined for great things. Only a lot of us get attacked and stopped before we can ever get started. Satan wants to stop us and crush us where we stand. But the good news is that he can't.

That is if we don't give up. We are difference makers. We belong to God. We are bought and paid for with the blood of Jesus. We may not be famous or well known in this world. But in the heavenly kingdom we are all very well known. Our prayers are heard! The heavenly saints cheer us on as we fight the good fight. We are a part of the greatest and most powerful army that ever was or will be! Our place in this highly esteemed force of power should be an honor and a humbling obligation. We are to be pursuing our God given goal! "Not that I have already obtained all this, or have already arrived at my goal, but I press on to take hold of that for which Christ Jesus took hold of me!" (Phil 3:12).

The woman knew that her journey with the Lord would lead her to mountain tops and in low valleys. She knew that God would lead her into deeper water, but that He would never leave her. It was her job to trust. It was her job to stay alert. It was her job to fight.

"Fight the good fight of faith. Take hold of the eternal life to which you were called when you made your good confession in the presence of many witnesses" (1 Tim 6:12).

We as Christians are all in this fight together, and we will need armor, special armor. God tells us to put on His armor.

Ephesians 6:10–18 says, "Finally, be strong in the Lord and in His mighty power. Put on the full armor of God, so that you can take your stand against the devil's schemes. For our struggle is not against flesh and blood, but against the rulers, against the authorities, against the powers of this dark world and against the spiritual forces of evil in the heavenly realms. Therefore put on the full armor of God, so that when the day of evil comes, you may be able to stand your ground, and after you have done everything, to stand. Stand firm then, with the BELT

OF TRUTH buckled around your waist, with the BREASTPLATE OF RIGHTEOUSNESS in place, and with your FEET FITTED IN READINESS that comes from the gospel of peace. In addition to all this, take up the SHIELD OF FAITH, with which you can extinguish all the flaming arrows of the evil one. Take the HELMET OF SALVATION and the SWORD OF THE SPIRIT, which is the word of God. And pray in the Spirit on all occasions with all kinds of prayers and requests. With this in mind, be alert and always keep on praying for all the Lord's people."

This armor will never let us down. The belt will never break. The breastplate won't tarnish. The helmet will stay secure. The shield cannot be penetrated. The shoes will not wear out. The sword will never be dulled and the prayers will always be heard. We must remember this and believe it. This is God's armor. It's supernatural.

God's armor will never have to be replaced. But, it must be put on. Every day, we need to remember to fight the good fight with our armor on. "Because you, dear children, are from God and have overcome them, because the One who is in you is greater than the one who is in the world" (1 John 4:4).

Jesus told us himself in John 16:33, "I have told you these things, so that in me you may have peace. In this world you will have trouble. But take heart! I have overcome the world."

In Daniel 10:12, God's servant Daniel was told, "Do not be afraid Daniel. Since the first day that you set your mind to gain understanding and to humble yourself before your God, your words were heard, and I have come in response to them." And in Judges 6:12, Gideon was told, "The Lord is with you mighty warrior." These truths tell us that we are very special to God. Our Lord hears us, is with us, and fights for us. What good news for the Special Agents of God! As you go through your life's mission, accept this blessing.

"May God Himself, the God of peace, sanctify you through and through. May your whole spirit, soul, and body be kept blameless at the coming of our Lord Jesus Christ. The one who calls you is faithful, and He will do it" (1 Thes 5:23–24).

Amen!

A Girl and Her Suitcase

From the time of conception, we start our journey home. As a daughter of God, I see myself pulling this suitcase along with me everywhere I go. I have had this "suitcase," so to speak all my life. It contains things, child-of-God things. Things from Him.

I remember my own children when they were small, and we would be packing for a trip. They would try to pack the craziest things to put in their suitcases. I would reason with them and suggest something else. We would take out the items that made no sense and replace them with ones that did. They were always happy to have the better item when they reached their destination.

That is how I see my life with our heavenly Father. I tend to pack my suitcase full of things, and God is looking and saying to me those make no sense!

A lot of the time I find myself packing guilt, worry, frustration, fear, jealousy, hatred, regret, anger, and pride just to name a few. I have these things stuffed in my suitcase, and I'm hauling this junk around. It's a burdensome and heavy job doing this, and I'm easily worn out from it!

When I finally start listening to the Lord, He lovingly reminds me that I don't need those things where I'm going. Why would I haul those things around here on earth when they don't exist in heaven? So, I take out the junk and replace it with useful things that I can actually use to benefit others and myself. Unfortunately, a lot of the time we tend to pack our suitcases full of these hurtful things not realizing that we are stuffing it full of toxins.

In Galatians 5:22, scripture tells us that the fruit of the Spirit is love, joy, peace, forbearance, kindness, goodness, faithfulness, gentleness, and self-control. We need these fruits in our suitcase at all times in order to live a productive life for God. In Galatians 5:25–26, God also tells us that since we live by the Spirit, let us keep in step with the Spirit. Let us not become conceited, provoking, and envying each other.

We have a choice what to put in our suitcases and what to leave out. We have a choice to either

haul the junk around, which just leads to more frustration and stress or call out to God to help us get rid of it once and for all. Your load will be much lighter and your journey so much better.

As you go through this life, try and pack your suitcase with things from and of God. When our journey is done here on earth, I pray that we all have suitcases bulging with things from the Father. Great things that make us more like Jesus!

CAMILA'S BALLOON

little girl released a balloon into the air one day. It happened to be on Valentine's Day. Her daddy had given it to her. It was a heart-shaped one with hearts and the word *love* written on it. The little girl wrote a note and taped it on the balloon. The note read, "Dear Jesus, I love you. Can you send a note back?" She included her address.

She walked into the living room where her daddy was sitting. She showed him the note and told him she was going to take it outside and send it to heaven. Her dad sat there trying to hold back the tears because he could see the sincere love for Jesus in his child. She truly expected a note back from Jesus. Every day she would run and check the mailbox after school.

She would ask her parents and her grandmother if they thought that Jesus would write her back. Her mother told her that she just had to believe. Days went by without a letter. Her grandmother phoned a friend and asked her if she might write the little girl a letter. At first her friend was a little taken aback by the request. But after she prayed and thought about the request, she decided to do it. She knew that the Lord had sent people with kind words just when she needed them, or a note from a friend that gave her comfort. Sometimes it might be through reading His word or hearing a sermon that she would hear His voice. What she did know was that the Lord was there. He heard her, and he talked back.

The friend sat down and typed out a letter to Camila. After she was done, she read it over and over. She knew that the letter was for her as well as the little girl. She knew that the letter would bless everyone who read it because it is how Jesus sees all of the children of God.

A lot of times we as Christians act and live as though we are waiting on a special letter from Jesus. We think if we could just have the Lord's words written especially for us, then we would know what to do, or we would take God more seriously. God already wrote us lots of letters. He gave us the Bible, which tells us everything we need to know to live this life victoriously. He didn't say it won't be hard, but He did say that we would be victorious.

Take a moment and read the letter to Camila. As you read it, see yourself as the little girl sending up the balloon in hopes of a letter. Hear the sweet words of our Savior saying that He is right here as close as the air you breathe.

A Love Letter

Dear Camila,

I saw your pretty balloon the other day. I smiled as I watched you release it into the air. *I love you too!* I always see you, and I hear your sweet, sweet prayers. You are my precious child. I hold you in my hand, and I will never let you go.

Please keep talking to me. I am always with you. Listen to the Holy Spirit, because He speaks my words. You don't need a letter from me because I speak directly to your heart. I am as close as the air you breathe. We are always able to talk. When you pray, I hear every word. I see every tear. I know every thought that you have. I see all, and I know all.

As you grow and become a beautiful young lady, don't forget to keep your childlike eyes on me. Through good times and bad times, I will never leave your side. You are my treasure, my beautiful and delicate rose. Nothing can take my love for you away.

Stand strong, little Camila. Always speak the truth about your Savior Jesus Christ. You will do great things in my name. Did you know that the little things are what I consider great things? Things like telling the truth, caring for others, speaking kind words, and sharing the good news that I died and rose again to give anyone who asks eternal life. I will bless you and your family beyond measure.

I take great delight in loving you! You are special.

Love,
The Savior of the world, *Jesus*

PS: I sent these words through another daughter of mine whom I also love. She knows how cherished you are to me as are all of my children. I spoke to her heart and told her to send you this letter for me.

The GIRL NAMED 23

The Girl Named
Twenty-Three

The young woman and her accomplice rushed into the small business. The unsuspecting business owners were busy picking paint colors for their remodeling project when the couple burst in telling them their wild tale. They explained how they desperately needed twenty-three dollars for bus fare to Tennessee. The woman told how she and her husband had been in an argument the night before, and she and her friend had asked to be let out of the car. She told them how they had wandered around all night and that they only needed twenty-three dollars to have enough bus fare to make it home.

The woman showed them her busted lip as she claimed that her husband had hit her the night before. When she finished with her desperate story, she stood there out of breath waiting for a response.

The business owners stood there wide-eyed trying to take in the whole story. The older woman opened her purse and started searching for twenty-three dollars. Soon she found the exact amount of money and took it to the younger woman. She handed it to her and looked deep into her tired brown eyes and told her that she hoped she was telling her the truth. In her heart, the godly woman knew that they were probably a couple of scammers, but she felt moved to give them the money anyway.

The young woman played her part like a pro. Insisting on hugging the older woman, she left her with a heavy scent of cigarettes and convenience store fried food.

As quickly as they had come they were gone, leaving the older woman feeling like she had been in a whirlwind. She felt a little silly for giving them the money. She didn't even get their names. In her mind, she imagined the man named James and the woman named Gina. For now, she would just call her Twenty-three, referring to the odd dollar amount that she asked for.

The couple jumped into the pickup truck waiting for them around the corner and headed straight for the casino. They laughed and complimented each other on the way each part was perfectly played. As soon as she hit the door, she headed for her favorite craps table and laid her twenty-three dollars down on the table. Twenty-three was her lucky number because it was her birthday.

"Winner!" the dealer yelled out.

She had doubled her money. Twenty-three hooted and hollered celebrating with a cigarette and a stiff drink. She just knew that one day she was going to win it big. Maybe it would be today, and life would be good.

The next morning, all the winnings she had left was one dollar and a headache. She didn't even have enough money for a cigarette.

That same morning, the older woman was drinking her coffee and having her quiet time with the Lord. She kept thinking about the girl she had named Twenty-three. She knew that God had put Twenty-three in her path for some reason. Maybe she was in desperate need of prayer. So, the godly woman decided that she was going to pray for Twenty-three and her friend every day. She began to pray for her right then.

She said, "Lord, only you can change this woman's heart and turn her life around. She needs you,

Lord. Help her and her friend, God, to see what is right and what is wrong. Send someone to her, Lord, to tell her about Jesus. In Jesus', name, amen."

Meanwhile, Twenty-three was down on her luck again and trying to figure out what scam she could pull off next. She took her dollar bill into the convenience store. The only thing she could afford was a pack of gum. She also slipped a drink and some chips inside her coat on the way to the checkout line.

When she left, two men followed her outside and held her there for shoplifting until the police came. They took her to the city jail and booked her. While she was there, they discovered that she was wanted on some other charges, so she was sentenced to jail for twenty-three days.

As she sat in her jail cell, she decided that maybe twenty-three wasn't her lucky number after all. Her mind faded back to better days in her life. How did she let herself get to this place? Why did her choices always seem to be wrong? As she lay back on her bed, she could see the face of the older woman who had given her the twenty-three dollars. She thought of how the woman had looked at her. Her eyes seemed to pierce her very soul. She remembered how she had told her that she hoped she was telling the truth. She knew that the older woman didn't believe her and the accomplice, but why did she help them anyway? She felt a little bad, but she convinced herself that the older woman would never miss the money.

Days passed and then weeks. On day 17 in jail, Twenty-three had a visitor. A local church had a jail ministry, and they would come and witness to the prisoners. The prisoners had the choice to come and listen to the people or to decline. The young woman decided that she would go and listen. She had been bored silly and could use some conversation.

She and some other prisoners were taken to a large room where four people in street clothes were waiting. An elderly woman with short white hair and shiny brown eyes came walking her way. She smiled at Twenty-three and looked at her. She asked her how she was doing and if she could visit with her for a while.

Twenty-three explained that she was being released in seven days. She told her that she had run into some bad luck. The elderly woman opened a small Bible and asked her if she could read some verses to her. Twenty-three agreed to let her read some verses. The young woman really didn't know much about the Bible. She supposed God was up there in heaven somewhere. He had never been much help to her although she never really asked him for it.

The woman started reading from Luke 15:3. It was a parable about a shepherd having one hundred sheep, and one of them gets lost. She told how the shepherd would leave the other ninety-nine sheep just to go and find the one lost sheep. And when he found it, he joyfully put it on his shoulders and went home. He called all of his friends and neighbors together for a celebration because he had found his lost sheep.

The woman carefully explained the parable to Twenty-three. She told her that the shepherd was Jesus, God's son, and that all of mankind are his sheep. She explained how so many people go through life lost and separated from Jesus and don't even know they are lost. All the while Jesus is searching and calling for his lost ones. He calls out to them, but they do not answer, because they don't know his voice.

She told Twenty-three how Jesus longed to take every lost person into his arms and save them from this world and their lives of sin. She explained how even if there was one lost person in this world, He would still come after them and bring them to his home.

The elderly woman looked at Twenty-three and asked her if she had ever asked Jesus to save her before. Twenty-three sat there, playing the story over in her mind again. Finally, she quietly said, "No, I haven't. Why would Jesus want to help me? I have never done anything for him?"

The elderly woman told her that it was because he loved her and wanted to set her free. The young woman thought to herself that all her life, that was all she wanted, to be *free*—free from the struggle, the bad decisions, the disappointments, the despair, the longing to have it all. The young woman had always run from one relationship to the next trying to find happiness and security. She tried all kinds of ways to find happiness by stealing, lying, cheating, alcohol, drugs, you name it. Yet she always came up short. She was still a young woman, but she felt and looked so old and tired. She was tired of the struggle. She wanted to have a good life, but she just couldn't seem to stay away from bad choices.

The elderly woman told her that God loved her and sent His only son Jesus to help her and to save her. He wanted to give her not only eternal life and riches in heaven, but also a life of peace and joy here on earth. She read to her John3:16: "For God so loved the world that He gave His one and only Son, that whoever believes in Him shall not perish but have eternal life."

She also read her John 10:9–11 when Jesus tells us, "I am the gate; whoever enters through me will be saved. They will come in and go out, and find pasture. The thief comes only to steal and kill and destroy; I have come that they may have life, and have it to the full. I am the good shepherd. The shepherd lays down his life for his sheep."

The visitation time was up. The guards came in to take the prisoners back to their cells. The elderly woman gave Twenty-three a small Bible and a bookmark. She encouraged her to read the book of John and the bookmark. She prayed a short prayer for Twenty-three before they took her away.

That night Twenty-three lay on her bed with her little Bible in her hands. She thumbed through it until she found John. She started reading about how Jesus was with God from the beginning and that through him all things were made. It said that in Jesus was life, and He was the light of all mankind and that nothing can overcome His light. She read on about John the Baptist and how Jesus had called his twelve disciples to follow him. She read John 3:16 that the woman had talked about.

Then she came to the story of the Samaritan woman. As she read it she could see herself, a woman with a checkered past. Jesus knew everything about

the woman at the well, yet He offered her water anyway, living water. She, in turn, told others about Jesus, and many were saved.

The woman read on about how Jesus healed people, turned water to wine, walked on water, and raised the dead. She read how Jesus lovingly washed his disciples' feet and predicted that one of them would betray him. She noticed Jesus's love for his disciples as he told them not to be troubled that he had to go away to prepare a place for them. She read how he promised to send the Holy Spirit so that no one would be alone. Jesus explained how the Holy Spirit would be our helper.

As she read on, she came to the part where Jesus was arrested, and his beloved disciple Peter denied him three times. She was saddened how Jesus was questioned and brutally beaten all night and eventually hung on the cross to die the next day. As the woman read on, she was amazed and glad that the tomb was found empty and that God had raised Jesus from the dead.

She loved the fact that his disciples got to see him again and that he forgave Peter for denying him. She noticed that at the end of the book, John claimed that if everyone had written down all of the great things that Jesus had done, there wouldn't be room in the world for the books that would have to be written!

Next, the woman picked up the bookmark and looked at it. It said to be joyful in hope. It stated that she was "fearfully and wonderfully made" (Ps 139:14). It also said that "the Lord was near to all who call on him. He hears their cry and saves them" (Ps 145:18–19). On the back of the bookmark it had the ABCs of becoming a Christian or a follower of Jesus. They were listed in order.

> *Admit.* Admit to God that you are a sinner. Repent and turn away from your sins. (Rom 6:23)
>
> *Believe.* Believe that Jesus is God's son and that God sent Jesus to save people from their sins. Jesus died on the cross and rose from the dead. (Rom 5:8)
>
> *Confess.* Confess you want Jesus to be Lord of your life and commit your life to Jesus. Trust Him to be your Lord and Savior. (Rom 10:9 and 13)

Then at the very bottom of the bookmark, it said, "Come to Me, all you who are weary and burdened, and I will give you rest" (Matt 11:28).

The woman lay there in the dark. Tears were running down her cheeks. She began to pray, "Oh God, I need your help. I do know that I'm a sinner. Help me God to turn away from this life. I do believe that Jesus is your Son and that he died to set me free. And, Lord, I confess that I want you to be Lord of my life. I trust you God. Please save me. Amen."

She fell asleep that night on her tear-stained pillow, but she didn't feel alone. She was truly happy for the first time in her life.

The six remaining days went by very quickly for Twenty-three. She would read her Bible every day. Finally, the day came for her release. She was leaving without a penny in her pocket and no one to call. As she stepped outside, she was surprised to see the elderly woman standing there. She told her that she thought that she might need a ride somewhere. The young woman cried and told her how she had asked Jesus to save her, and He did! They hugged, and they cried.

The elderly woman told her about a Christian shelter that helped women get a job and a place to live. Twenty-three jumped at the chance. She knew that God was helping her to start this new life over again, and she was grateful.

As time went by, Twenty-three found a job and eventually a small apartment. She started attending church and going to Bible studies. She was so happy, because she was finally free. One day after work, she knew that there was something that God was wanting her to do. She needed to go and give the twenty-three dollars back to the kind woman.

As she stepped inside the newly remodeled waiting room, the older woman didn't recognize her. She was clean and nicely dressed. Her hair was pretty and shiny, and her eyes were bright and full of life.

She asked, "May I help you?"

Twenty-three walked toward her with tears in her eyes and said, "I have come to return your twenty-three dollars that you gave to me and my friend a year ago."

The woman looked at her closely and, smiling, said, "Well, hello, Twenty-three. I didn't recognize you! I never knew your name, so I've been calling you Twenty-three when I prayed for you. I just prayed for you this morning. It looks like to me that it may have done some good!"

"Yes, it did," she replied. "And by the way, my name is Jenny."

Jenny told her how she had gambled the money away and how she had spent time in jail for other mistakes. She told her how a nice lady had told her about Jesus and had given her a Bible while she was in jail. She explained how she had accepted Jesus as her Savior and how He had turned her life around.

She handed the woman the twenty-three dollars and said that God wanted her to make it right. The older woman said that it was money well spent if it brought her to Jesus. She told Jenny how she had prayed for her and her friend to find the Lord. She asked her about her friend.

Jenny told her that he liked his old life and thought that hers was silly. She told her that she had to give up most of her friends to follow Jesus but that she had made so many new ones who loved Jesus. Jenny hugged the older woman good-bye and promised that she would stop in again and say hello. This time the woman could only smell the light scent of flowers mixed with Jesus. What a great combination.

When Jenny left, the older woman wept as she held the twenty-three dollars. She thanked God that her prayers, for Twenty-three had not been in vain. She praised Him for the miracle that she had just witnessed. She also decided that she was not going to give up on the young man whom she had named

James. Tomorrow morning, she and her coffee would go to battle again in the name of the Lord.

> The Lord is my shepherd, I lack nothing. He makes me lie down in green pastures, he leads me beside quiet waters, he refreshes my soul. He guides me along the right paths for his name's sake. Even though I walk through the darkest valley, I will fear no evil, for you are with me; your rod and your staff, they comfort me. You prepare a table before me in the presence of my enemies. You anoint my head with oil; my cup overflows. Surely your goodness and love will follow me all the days of my life, and I will dwell in the house of the Lord forever. (Ps 23:1–6)

LET YOUR FLOWER BLOOM

*B*eloved, have you ever thought of yourself as a beautiful flower in the dark tapestry of life? As Christians, we are continually blooming and spreading sweet aromas for others around us to see and breathe in. Our fragrant and colorful blooms burst forth and give life to this darkened world. Our petals are ever so soft and healing to others. Our petals so to speak are our words, thoughts, actions, and deeds as they are guided and directed by the sweet Holy Spirit.

As you go through each day, think of yourself as a lovely flower. Plant your roots deep into God's word. Rejoice as He sends you showers of blessings to quench the dry soil where you stand. Raise your beautiful face to Jesus and receive His beneficial sunlight, which enables you to thrive and grow strong.

Drink in precious nutrients as you pray and seek counsel from the Holy Spirit.

As we all know, the circumstances of life sometimes cause our flower to bend. We might even lose some of our petals or become withered. On occasion our bloom may even break and fall away. We might experience periods of drought, or the sun might be blocked from our view.

Thankfully, these moments won't last forever. The beautiful One sees to it that we are tended to. As we stand in hope and faith, our God in His ever–loving-kindness makes us strong again. The tender care of God's powerful hand soothes and cradles us. Before long a tiny bud reappears, and soon we are in full bloom again.

In 2 Corinthians 2:14–15, the scripture says, "But thanks be to God, who always leads us in triumphal procession in Christ and through us spreads everywhere the fragrance of the knowledge of Him. For we are to God the aroma of Christ to those who are being saved and those who are perishing."

The Lord is looking to us to share His beauty with others. So, every day stand ready with your glorious blooms spreading sweet aromas and blessing those in need. Let your beauty burst forth and show others the love of Christ, because together we all make a lovely bouquet.

ABOUT THE AUTHOR

This book is Andi Whitefield's first attempt in the literary world. A retired elementary school teacher, Andi has always dreamed of writing books.

Andi is married to her high school sweetheart, Quint, and has two adult children, Drew and Taylor.

CPSIA information can be obtained
at www.ICGtesting.com
Printed in the USA
FSOW04n1250051017
39562FS